Thank you to the generous team who gave their time and talents to make this book possible:

Author
Worku L. Mulat

Illustrator
Daniel Getahun

Creative Directors
Caroline Kurtz, Jane Kurtz, and Kenny Rasmussen

Translator
Worku L. Mulat

Designers
Beth Crow and Kenny Rasmussen

Ready Set Go Books, an Open Hearts Big Dreams Project

Special thanks to Ethiopia Reads donors and staff for believing in this project and helping get it started-- and for arranging printing, distribution, and training in Ethiopia.

ISBN: 979-8553404970
Library of Congress Control Number: 2020917970

Republished: 10/26/20

ተስፋ ያልቆረጠው ልጅ!

The Boy Who Never Gave Up!

English and Amharic

The boy who grew up to be
Saint Yared was born in
Axum about 1500 years ago.

ከብዙ ዓመታት በፊት ተወልዶ በኋላ
ቅዱስ ያሬድ የሆነው ልጅ ዕድገቱ
አክሱም ነበር።

His early life was hard. Both of his parents died when he was seven years old. An uncle took him in and sent him to school to learn from the priests who taught boys to read.

: የያሬድ የልጅነት ጊዜ ችግር የተሞላበት ነበር። እናትና አባቱ ከዚህ ዓለም በሞት የተለዩበት ጊዜ የ7ዓመት ልጅ እያለ ነበር። ስለዚህ አጎቱ ንባብ እንዲማር በማሰብ ወሰዱትና ሕፃናት ወደሚያስተምሩ መሪጌታዎች ላኩት።

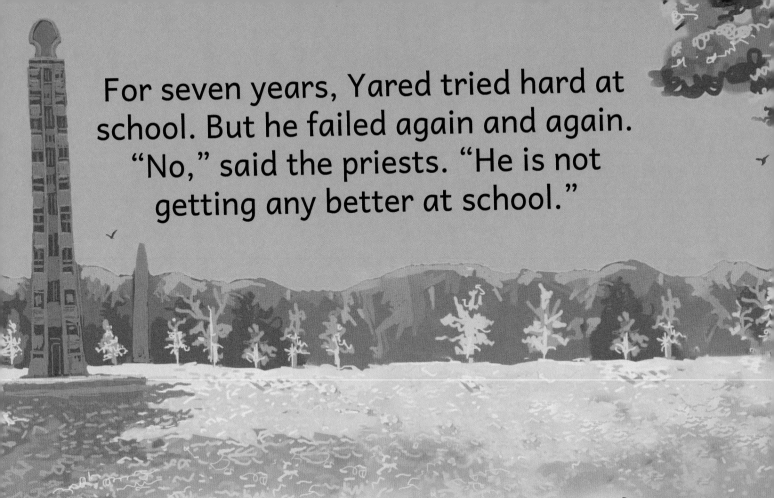

For seven years, Yared tried hard at school. But he failed again and again. "No," said the priests. "He is not getting any better at school."

ያሬድ በሚችለው አቅሙ ትምህርቱን ለ ሰባት ዓመታት ተከታተለ። ሆኖም ግን በተደጋጋሚ ወደቀ። በዚህ ጊዜ መሪጌታው "በቃ ያሬድ ትምህርቱ ሊገባው አልቻለም" አሉ።

"What will help this boy?" his uncle thundered. "Shall I beat him?" Yared's heart was a tangle of frustration. He ran away.

"ይህ ልጅ ምን ይሻለዋል?" ብለው አጎቱ ብስጭት አሉ። "ልግረፈው ይሆን?"። ያሬድ በእጅጉ ተስፋ ቆረጠ። ያጎቱን ቤት ጥሎ ኮበለለ።

Yared ran and ran.
He ran until he dropped under a tree.
So tired! So frustrated!

ያሬድ ያለማቋረጥ ሮጠ። ደክሞት ከአንድ ዛፍ
ጥላ ሥር እስከሚያርፍ ሩጫውን ቀጠለ።
በጣም ደከመ፤ በእጅጉ ተስፋ ቆረጠ።

Above his head, he saw a caterpillar
trying to crawl up the tree trunk.
The caterpillar failed again and again.
One... two... three... four... five... six.

ቀና ብሎ ሲመለከት አንዲት ትል በዛፉ ግንድ ላይ
እየተሳበች ከጫፍ ለመድረስ ስትታገል አየ።
ትሏ በተደጋጋሚ ስትወድቅ ተመለከተ።
አንድ... ሁለት... ሶስት... አራት... አምስት... ስድስት።

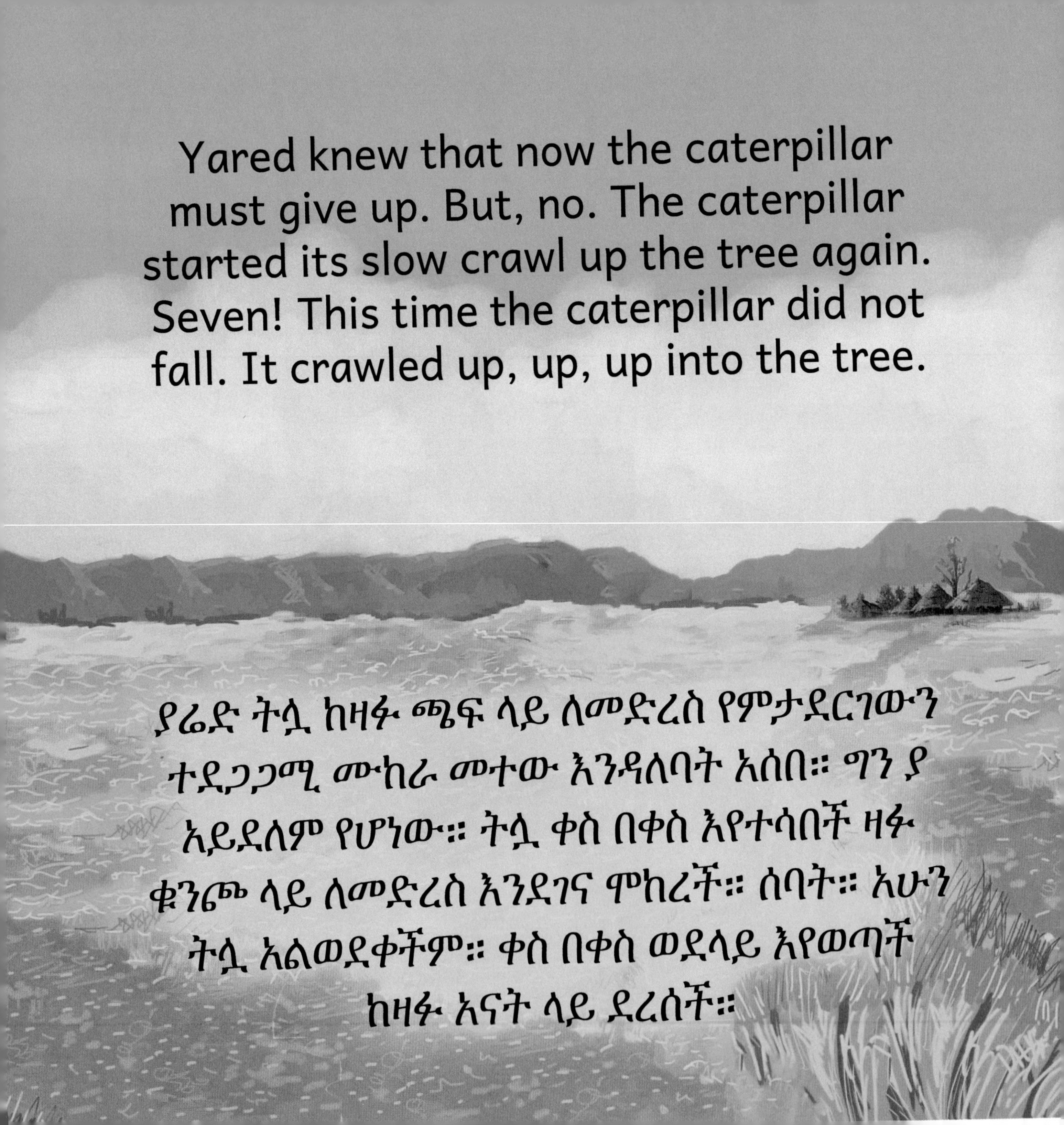

Yared knew that now the caterpillar must give up. But, no. The caterpillar started its slow crawl up the tree again. Seven! This time the caterpillar did not fall. It crawled up, up, up into the tree.

ያሬድ ትሏ ከዛፉ ጫፍ ላይ ለመድረስ የምታደርገውን ተደጋጋሚ ሙከራ መተው እንዳለባት አሰበ። ግን ያ አይደለም የሆነው። ትሏ ቀስ በቀስ እየተሳበች ዛፉ ቁንጮ ላይ ለመድረስ እንደገና ሞከረች። ሰባት። አሁን ትሏ አልወደቀችም። ቀስ በቀስ ወደላይ እየወጣች ከዛፉ አናት ላይ ደረሰች።

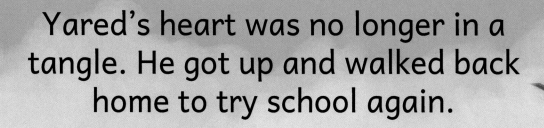

Yared's heart was no longer in a
tangle. He got up and walked back
home to try school again.

አሁን የያሬድ ልብ በተስፋ መቁረጥ
አልተሞላም። ካረፈበት የዛፍ ጥላ
ስር ተነስቶ ወደ አንቱ ቤት ተመለሰ።
ትምህርቱንም ለመቀጠል ወሰነ።

This time, he stayed with his studies until he was able to drink in the many sacred books and the laws of the church. He became the strongest student of all.

ከዚያ በኋላ ቅዱሳን መጽሐፍትን እና ቤተ ክርስቲያን የምትተዳደርበትን ህግ ጠንቅቆ እስከሚያጠና ድረስ በትምህርት ቤት ቆየ። በዘመኑ ከነበሩት ተማሪዎች ሁሉ በትምህርቱ ብልጫ አሳየ።

In the end, Yared--who once failed again and again--became Saint Yared because of his great gift for inventing a way to write church music.

በመጨረሻም በተደጋጋሚ ይወድቅ የነበረው ትንሹ ልጅ ያሬድ በኋላ ባገኘው የቤተክርስቲያን ዜማን የመድረስ ስጦታ ቅዱስ ያሬድ ለመባል በቃ።

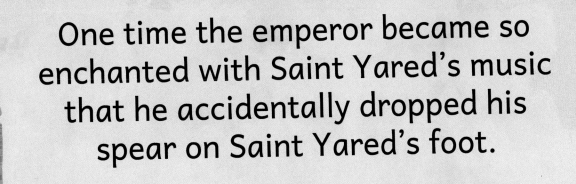

One time the emperor became so enchanted with Saint Yared's music that he accidentally dropped his spear on Saint Yared's foot.

የቅዱስ ያሬድ ዜማ እጅግ መሳጭ ከመሆኑ የተነሳ ንጉሡ ይዘውት የነበረውን ጦር ሳያውቁት ቅዱስ ያሬድ እግር ላይ ሰኩት።

Saint Yared's hymns were a gift
passed down to many generations.
The world is thankful this boy became
a strong student and then a musician
and then a saint because he learned
never to give up.

የቅዱስ ያሬድ ዜማ ከትውልድ ወደ ትውልድ
ሲተላለፍ የሚኖር ድንቅ ገጸ በረከት ነው፡፡
ይህ ልጅ በመጀመሪያ ጠንካራ ተማሪ፣ ቀጥሎ
ዜማ ደራሲ፣ በመጨረሻ ቅዱስ ያሬድ ለመሆን
በመብቃቱ ዓለም ምስጋና ታቀርብለታለች፡፡

About The Story

The boy who became Saint Yared grew up in the ancient kingdom of Axum. According to legend, he struggled as a student, just as this story shows, but eventually triumphed and went on to invent Ethiopia's system of musical notation. His work drew on local traditions and the church concept of the Holy Trinity, while his hymns had four parts based on the four seasons of the year, winter, summer, spring, and autumn. Hundreds of years before European composers developed a seven-note system of writing music, Yared wrote music using dashes, curves, and dots to represent ten different notes. The website Black Past says that although he is not well known outside of Ethiopia, Saint Yared was "a major innovator in the development of medieval music."

About The Author

Worku L. Mulat joined the Ready Set Go Books team early in 2019, first as a translator and now as an author. He holds a PhD from University College Cork in Ireland, an MSc from Gent University, Belgium, and a BSc from Asmara University, Eritrea. Dr. Worku has published extensively professional articles on high impact journals such as Malaria Journal, Environmental Monitoring and Assessment, Ecological Indicators, Bioresource Technology, and PLOS ONE. He also co-authored three books with a main theme of Environmental conservation. Currently he is working for Open Hearts Big Dreams Fund as Innovation Center Lead in Model projects being implemented in Ethiopia. He is also a research associate at Tree Foundation which strives to save Ethiopian Orthodox church forests.

About The Illustrator

Daniel Getahun lives in Toronto, Canada. He received a diploma in graphic art from Addis Ababa School of Fine Arts and Design in 1980. He now focuses on oil painting and digital painting, which can be seen on his Facebook page. He can also be contacted by email: danielgetahun1@hotmail.com

About Open Hearts Big Dreams

Open Hearts Big Dreams began as a volunteer organization, led by Ellenore Angelidis in Seattle, Washington, to provide sustainable funding and strategic support to Ethiopia Reads, collaborating with Jane Kurtz. OHBD has now grown to be its own nonprofit organization supporting literacy, innovation, and leadership for young people in Ethiopia.

Ellenore Angelidis comes from a family of teachers who believe education is a human right, and opportunity should not depend on your birthplace. And as the adoptive mother of a little girl who was born in Ethiopia and learned to read in the U.S., as well as an aspiring author, she finds the chance to positively impact literacy hugely compelling!

About Ready Set Go Books

Reading has the power to change lives, but many children and adults in Ethiopia cannot read. One reason is that Ethiopia doesn't have enough books in local languages to give people a chance to practice reading.

Ready Set Go books wants to close that gap and open a world of ideas and possibilities for kids and their communities.

When you buy a Ready Set Go book, you provide critical funding to create and distribute more books.

Learn more at: http://openheartsbigdreams.org/book-project/

Ready Set Go 10 Books

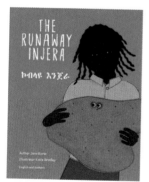

In 2018, Ready Set Go Books decided to experiment by trying a few new books in larger sizes.

Sometimes it was the art that needed a little more room to really shine. Sometimes the story or nonfiction text was a bit more complicated than the short and simple text used in most of our current early reader books.

We called these our "Ready Set Go 10" books as a way to show these ones are bigger and also sometimes have more words on the page. The response has been great so now our Ready Set Go 10 books are a significant number of our titles. We are happy to hear feedback on these new books and on all our books.

About the Language

Amharic is a Semetic language -- in fact, the world's second-most widely spoken Semetic language, after Arabic. Starting in the 12th century, it became the Ethiopian language that was used in official transactions and schools and became widely spoken all over Ethiopia. It's written with its own characters, over 260 of them. Eritrea and Ethiopia share this alphabet, and they are the only countries in Africa to develop a writing system centuries ago that is still in use today!

About the Translation

Worku L. Mulat joined the translation team of Ready Set Go Books early in 2019. He holds a PhD from University College Cork in Ireland, an MSc from Gent University, Belgium, and a BSc from Asmara University, Eritrea. Dr. Worku has published extensively professional articles on high impact journals such as Malaria Journal, Environmental Monitoring and Assessment, Ecological Indicators, Bioresource Technology, and PLOS ONE. He also co-authored three books with a main theme of Environmental conservation. Currently he is working for Open Hearts Big Dreams Fund as Innovation Center Lead in Model projects being implemented in Ethiopia. He is also a research associate at Tree Foundation which strives to save Ethiopian Orthodox church forests.

Find more Ready Set Go Books on Amazon.com

To view all available titles, search "Ready Set Go Ethiopia" or scan QR code

 Chaos

 Talk Talk Turtle

 The Glory of Gondar

 We Can Stop the Lion

 Not Ready!

 Fifty Lemons

 Count For Me

 Too Brave

 Tell Me What You Hear

Made in the USA
Monee, IL
23 December 2020